SALINA LIBRARY
100 BELMONT STREET
MATTYDALE, NY 13211
315-454-4524

JUNIOR BIOS

Tom Holland

BY NORA GARDINER

Please visit our website, www.enslow.com. For a free color catalog of all our high-quality books, call toll free 1-800-398-2504 or fax 1-877-980-4454.

Library of Congress Cataloging-in-Publication Data

Names: Gardiner, Nora, author.
Title: Tom Holland / Nora Gardiner.
Description: New York : Enslow Publishing, [2022] | Series: Junior bios | Includes index.
Identifiers: LCCN 2020037620 (print) | LCCN 2020037621 (ebook) | ISBN 9781978522763 (library binding) | ISBN 9781978522749 (paperback) | ISBN 9781978522756 (6 pack) | ISBN 9781978522770 (ebook)
Subjects: LCSH: Holland, Tom, 1996- —Juvenile literature. | Actors—Great Britain—Biography—Juvenile literature. | Dancers—Great Britain—Biography—Juvenile literature.
Classification: LCC PN2598.H58 G37 2022 (print) | LCC PN2598.H58 (ebook) | DDC 791.4302/8092 [B]—dc23
LC record available at https://lccn.loc.gov/2020037620
LC ebook record available at https://lccn.loc.gov/2020037621

First Edition

Published in 2022 by
Enslow Publishing
29 E. 21st Street
New York, NY 10010

Copyright © 2022 Enslow Publishing

Designer: Deanna Paternostro
Editor: Kate Mikoley

Photo credits: Cover, p. 1 (Tom Holland) Mike Marsland/Contributor/WireImage/Getty Images; cover, p. 1 (photo frame) Aleksandr Andrushkiv/Shutterstock.com; marble texture used throughout HardtIllustrations/Shutterstock.com; lined paper texture used throughout Mtsaride/Shutterstock.com; watercolor texture used throughout solarbird/Shutterstock.com; p. 5 Jason LaVeris/Contributor/FilmMagic/Getty Images; pp. 7, 10 David M. Benett/Contributor/Getty Images Entertainment/Getty Images; p. 9 Kevork Djansezian/Stringer/Getty Images Entertainment/Getty Images; p. 13 Jason Merritt/TERM/Staff/Getty Images Entertainment/Getty Images; pp. 15, 16 David M. Benett/Contributor/WireImage/Getty Images; p. 17 Jamie McCarthy/Staff/Getty Images Entertainment/Getty Images; p. 19 Bobby Bank/Contributor/GC Images/Getty Images.

All rights reserved. No part of this book may be reproduced in any form without permission in writing from the publisher, except by a reviewer.

Printed in the United States of America

CPSIA compliance information: Batch #CSENS22: For further information contact Enslow Publishing, New York, New York, at 1-800-398-2504.

Find us on f ⌾

Contents

Getting Started 4
All in the Family 6
Dancing into the Spotlight 8
Moving On to Movies 12
Stepping into Spider-Man 14
It's Tom's Time! 20
Tom's Timeline 21
Glossary 22
For More Information 23
Index 24

Words in the glossary appear in **bold** type the first time they are used in the text.

Getting Started

When you hear Tom Holland's name, you likely think of his role as Peter Parker—or Spider-Man—in the popular Marvel movies. Perhaps you remember him from one of his other movie roles. If you're a superfan, maybe you've seen enough **interviews** with him that you just think of Tom as himself.

Whatever you think of when you think of Tom Holland, it's probably not an image of a young boy taking a hip-hop dance class. But when he was a child, that's exactly what Tom was doing! In fact, it's what led him to his start in acting.

TOM FIRST APPEARED AS SPIDER-MAN IN THE 2016 MOVIE CAPTAIN AMERICA: CIVIL WAR.

All in the Family

Tom was born on June 1, 1996, near London, England. His mom, Nicola, is a **photographer**. His dad, Dominic, is a comedian, or a person who tells jokes in front of groups of people. He's also an author.

FACTS BEHIND THE FIGURE

In 2012, Tom started at the BRIT School. This is a special school in England that focuses on performing arts. Many famous artists went there, such as Adele and Jessie J.

Tom, Dominic, Paddy, Nicola, Sam, and Harry Holland

TOM'S FAMILY HAS BEEN THERE THROUGHOUT HIS SUCCESS. HE'S SAID HE'S LEARNED FROM HIS DAD'S EXPERIENCE IN THE ENTERTAINMENT **INDUSTRY**.

Tom has three younger brothers: Harry, Sam, and Paddy. They've each done a bit of their own acting too. Harry and Tom sometimes work together. Harry even worked as an assistant on the crew of *Spider-Man: Far from Home* (2019). In 2020, Tom said the two brothers were working on writing a **script** for a movie together.

Dancing into the Spotlight

When Tom was just a baby, his mom noticed he'd dance when certain songs were played. It wasn't long before he started taking dance classes.

When he was 10 years old, Tom's hip-hop class performed at a dance show. Talent scouts, or people whose job it is to find skilled performers, noticed Tom at the show! The scouts asked Tom to try out, or audition, for a show called *Billy Elliot the Musical*. The musical is based on a movie from 2000. It's about a boy who secretly starts taking dance classes even though he's supposed to be taking boxing classes.

TOM IS ALSO SKILLED AT GYMNASTICS, A SPORT THAT INCLUDES ROLLS, FLIPS, AND OTHER MOVES.

FACTS BEHIND THE FIGURE

Not everyone at the *Billy Elliot the Musical* audition thought Tom did a good job. At the time, he hadn't had any real acting experience. He'd also never done ballet, the type of dancing in the show. But the **director** thought he was a natural performer.

TOM'S PRODUCTIONS OF *BILLY ELLIOT THE MUSICAL* WERE IN LONDON'S WEST END. THIS IS AN AREA KNOWN FOR BIG THEATER PRODUCTIONS, SIMILAR TO BROADWAY IN NEW YORK.

Tom had to go through eight auditions before getting a role, or part, in *Billy Elliot the Musical*. Plus, he had to take ballet lessons for around two years! In June 2008, Tom finally appeared in his first performance of the show. At first, he played the main character's best friend, named Michael. Just a few months later, he started playing the main character—Billy!

Many actors have played Billy Elliot since the show started in London in 2005. Each actor has their own style. Tom became known for his gymnastic skills while playing Billy. Crowds were often impressed with his flips!

FACTS BEHIND THE FIGURE

Tom starred in the musical for nearly two years. His last performance playing Billy in the popular London show was on May 29, 2010, just a few days before he turned 14.

Moving On to Movies

Soon after leaving his role as Billy, Tom landed another role. This time, he wasn't dancing and singing onstage. Instead, he was doing the voice for a character in a British **animated** movie called *The Secret World of Arrietty*.

Also shortly after playing Billy, Tom was cast in a lead part in a movie called *The Impossible*. The movie came out in 2012. It was his work in this movie that made many people in the movie business notice Tom's skill for acting. He was **nominated** for several awards for his performance.

THE IMPOSSIBLE IS BASED ON A TRUE STORY OF A FAMILY CAUGHT IN A TSUNAMI. TOM PLAYED THE FAMILY'S OLDEST SON.

FACTS BEHIND THE FIGURE

Tom won several of the awards he was nominated for with The Impossible, such as the Hollywood Spotlight Award. The movie was first shown at a world-famous event called the Toronto Film Festival.

13

Stepping into Spider-Man

After *The Impossible*, Tom went on to act in several more movies. Soon, he landed a role that would make him the superstar he is today—Peter Parker, also known as Spider-Man.

In His Own Words

"I have always been a huge fan of Spider-Man, and growing up, I had countless Spider-Man costumes … He's always been a big part of my life and a big part of boys' lives because everybody can relate to him."

TOM'S PART IN *CAPTAIN AMERICA: CIVIL WAR* WAS FAIRLY SMALL, BUT IT WAS JUST THE START OF HIS ROLE IN MARVEL MOVIES!

Similar to when he tried out for *Billy Elliot the Musical*, Tom auditioned to play Spider-Man eight times. The process took about five months. Then, in June 2015, Marvel announced that he got the part. Tom says he found out the same way many fans did—he saw Marvel's post on Instagram! In 2016, he officially **launched** his career as Spider-Man when *Captain America: Civil War* came out.

15

In 2017, Tom was back on screen as Spider-Man. This time, he was the star! In the movie *Spider-Man: Homecoming*, Peter Parker tries to balance his regular life as a high school student with his secret life as a superhero. Lots of people liked the movie, and Tom won his first Teen Choice Award for it.

While Tom's Spider-Man is **live-action**, he's done his share of voice acting too. In 2019, he voiced a character in an animated movie called *Spies in Disguise*. In 2020, he was in *Onward* and *Dolittle*. Tom's Avengers costar Robert Downey Jr. starred in *Dolittle*.

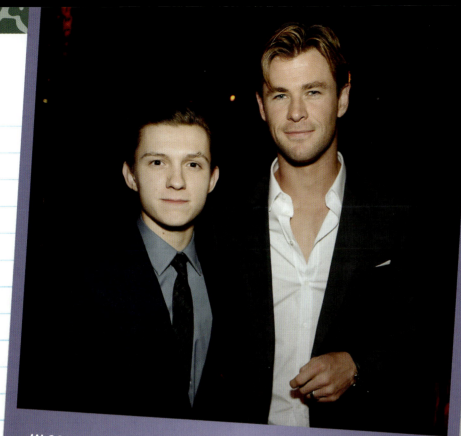

IN 2015, TOM WAS IN A MOVIE CALLED *IN THE HEART OF THE SEA* WITH CHRIS HEMSWORTH. THEY WORKED TOGETHER AGAIN IN THE AVENGERS MOVIES, IN WHICH CHRIS PLAYS THOR.

The Avengers are a team of Marvel superheroes who work together to fight their enemies. In 2018, Tom returned to the screen as Peter Parker/Spider-Man in *Avengers: Infinity War*. He was back again in 2019's *Avengers: Endgame*.

Just a few months after *Avengers: Endgame* came out, Tom was back on the big screen once again as Peter Parker in *Spider-Man: Far from Home*. By now, fans were used to seeing Tom play Spider-Man, but it was only his second time playing the character in a film where he was the star. Once again, his performance put him in the running for several awards. Among his wins were a Teen Choice Award and the Kids' Choice Award for favorite superhero.

In His Own Words

"The most important thing, in anything you do, is always trying your hardest, because even if you try your hardest and it's not as good as you'd hoped, you still have that sense of not letting yourself down."

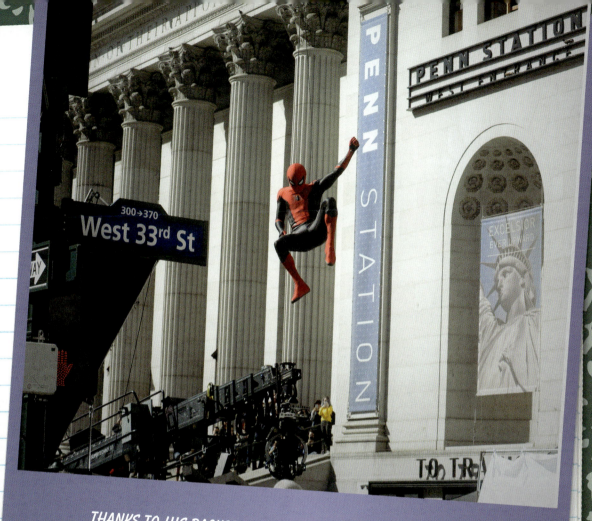

THANKS TO HIS BACKGROUND IN GYMNASTICS, TOM HAS BEEN ABLE TO DO MANY OF HIS OWN STUNTS IN THE SPIDER-MAN MOVIES.

Soon after *Spider-Man: Far from Home* came out, it was announced that Tom would be back to star in a third Spider-Man movie.

It's Tom's Time!

Between playing Spider-Man and acting in other movies, Tom's a busy guy. But he makes sure to leave time for other things too. Tom likes to spend time with his friends and family. He also loves to golf.

In 2017, Tom's parents started a group called the Brothers Trust, supported by all four Holland brothers. Through the group, Tom holds special events and helps raise money for charities.

Someday, Tom would like to do more than act in movies. He'd like to direct them too. Will this star's future be as super as the hero he plays on screen? It's probably a safe bet!

Tom's Timeline

1996: Tom is born on June 1.

2006: Tom is asked to audition for *Billy Elliot the Musical*.

2008: Tom first appears in, and later stars in, *Billy Elliot the Musical*.

2010: Tom is in his last performance as Billy Elliot.

2012: *The Impossible* comes out.

2015: *In the Heart of the Sea* comes out.

2016: Tom plays Spider-Man for the first time in *Captain America: Civil War*.

2017: Tom stars in *Spider-Man: Homecoming*.

2018: *Avengers: Infinity War* comes out.

2019: *Avengers: Endgame* and *Spider-Man: Far From Home* come out.

Tom voices a character in the animated movie *Spies in Disguise*.

2020: Tom voices characters in the movies *Onward* and *Dolittle*.

Glossary

animated Consisting of drawings or computer images that appear to move.
director A person in charge of a movie, play, or other performance.
industry A group of businesses or people providing a similar service.
interview A meeting, often between a famous person and a reporter, at which people ask questions and get information.
launch To begin.
live-action Using actors and sets, rather than animation.
nominate To suggest someone for an honor.
photographer A person who takes pictures with a camera.
script A written plan for a movie or show.
tsunami A huge wave of water created by an underwater earthquake or volcano.

For More Information

Books

Kawa, Katie. *Tom Holland Is Spider-Man*. New York, NY: Gareth Stevens Publishing, 2020.

Orr, Nicole. *Tom Holland*. Kennett Square, PA: Purple Toad Publishing, 2018.

Websites

Peter Parker: Spider-Man
www.marvel.com/characters/spider-man-peter-parker
Find out more about the character Tom plays on Marvel's official website.

Tom Holland Biography
www.biography.com/actor/tom-holland
Read more about Tom's life and work on this website.

Publisher's note to educators and parents: Our editors have carefully reviewed these websites to ensure that they are suitable for students. Many websites change frequently, however, and we cannot guarantee that a site's future contents will continue to meet our high standards of quality and educational value. Be advised that students should be closely supervised whenever they access the internet.

Index

Avengers, 16, 17, 18
Avengers: Endgame, 17, 18
Avengers: Infinity War, 17
awards, 12, 13, 16, 18
Billy Elliot the Musical, 8, 9, 10, 11, 12, 15
BRIT School, 6
Brothers Trust, 20
Captain America: Civil War, 5, 15
dance classes, 4, 8, 9, 10
Dolittle, 16
Downey, Robert, Jr., 16
family, 6, 7, 20
gymnastics, 9, 11, 19
Hemsworth, Chris, 17

Holland, Harry, 7
Impossible, The, 12, 13, 14
In the Heart of the Sea, 17
Marvel, 4, 15, 17
Onward, 16
Secret World of Arrietty, The, 12
Spider-Man, 4, 5, 14, 15, 16, 17, 18, 19, 20
Spider-Man: Far from Home, 7, 18, 19
Spider-Man: Homecoming, 16
Spies in Disguise, 16
stunts, 19